DIVE IN THE VAMPIRE BUND

1

NOZOMU TAMAKI

Per me si va ne la città dolente,

per me si va ne l'etterno dolore,

per me si va tra la perduta gente.

Giustizia mosse il mio alto fattore:

fecemi la divina podestate,

la somma sapïenza e 'l primo amore.

Dinanzi a me non fuor cose create

se non etterne, e io etterno duro.

... ...za, voi ch'entrate.

... into the city of woe:
... into eternal pain:
... people lost for aye.

Justice the founder of my fabric mov'd:
To rear me was the task of power divine,
Supremest wisdom, and primeval love.

Before me, things create were none, save things
Eternal, and eternal I shall endure.
All hope abandon, ye who enter here.

−Dante's Inferno, Canto III

Dive in the Vampire Bund
VOLUME 1

story & art by Nozomu Tamaki

STAFF CREDITS

translation **Adrienne Beck**
adaptation **Janet Houck**
lettering **Roland Amago**
layout **Bambi Eloriaga-Amago,**
Alexis Roberts
cover design **Nicky Lim**
proofreader **Shanti Whitesides**
editor **Adam Arnold**

publisher **Jason DeAngelis**
Seven Seas Entertainment

DIVE IN THE VAMPIRE BUND VOL. 1
Copyright © 2010 by Nozomu Tamaki
First published in Japan in 2010 by MEDIA FACTORY, Inc. English translation
rights reserved by Seven Seas Entertainment, LLC. under the license from
MEDIA FACTORY, Inc., Tokyo.

ISBN: 978-1-626920-17-0
Printed in Canada
First Printing: October 2013
10 9 8 7 6 5 4 3 2 1

Seven Seas

FOLLOW US ONLINE: www.gomanga.com

READING DIRECTIONS

This book reads from *right to left*, Japanese style.
If this is your first time reading manga, you start
reading from the top right panel on each page and
take it from there. If you get lost, just follow the
numbered diagram here. It may seem backwards
at first, but you'll get the hang of it! Have fun!!

ON THIS TOUR, YOU WILL SET FOOT INSIDE THE ONE REGION IN THE ENTIRE WORLD WHERE VAMPIRES MAY LIVE FREELY AND OPENLY.

LADIES AND GENTLEMEN, WELCOME TO THE VAMPIRE BUND GUIDED TOUR!!

THE BLUND COVERS AN AREA OF APPROXIMATELY 1,651 HECTARES.

LITERALLY A CITY CONSTRUCTED ATOP THE SEA, ITS POPULATION OF 100,000 IS COMPRISED OF VAMPIRES FROM ALL CULTURES AND ETHNIC BACKGROUNDS...

MAN, WHAT THE HELL?

I DON'T SEE A SINGLE BLOODSUCKER ANYWHERE. BOR~RIING!

WELL, DUH. IT'S STILL DAYLIGHT.

AND NOW, WE WILL TAKE A SHORT REST BREAK. OUR SHOPS HAVE MANY SOUVE- NIRS...

Wait in the bathroom until sunset.

WELL ?

AT THE TOP.

GIFT SHOP, POSTCARD RACK...

SEE?

THEN I'M GONNA LIVE HARD, FAST, AND BIG!

HELL, YEAH! I'M SAYIN' GOODBYE TO THIS DULL-ASS *HUMAN* LIFE, AND GETTIN' ME A NEW ONE AS A VAMPIRE.

YEAH?

MASAKI...?

YOU'RE *SURE* YOU WANT TO BECOME A VAMPIRE...?

HUH?

QUIT TALKING OUT OF YOUR ASS, MAN.

IT WAS YOU, WASN'T IT?

LAST WEEK, THE BOSS OF "SERPI-ENTES" WENT DOWN. STABBED.

WE SHOULD GO HOME. TURN YOURSELF IN TO THE COPS...

RUNNING AND TRYING TO HIDE HERE ISN'T GOING TO SOLVE ANYTHING.

NOW THE WHOLE GANG IS OUT FOR THE HEAD OF THE GUY WHO DID IT.

WHAT'S THAT SUP-POSED TO MEAN...?

NOK NOK

'SIDES, YOU AREN'T EXACTLY CLEAN YOUR-SELF.

HELL, NO! I AIN'T GOING ANYWHERE NEAR NO PIGS!

THE SUN WENT DOWN AGES AGO.

WHAT'RE YOU TWO KIDS DOIN', HANGING OUT IN THE MEN'S ROOM?

ONE. HE IS.

I'M JUST ALONG FOR THE RIDE.

SO YOU TWO ARE THE ONES LOOKING TO GET TURNED?

YO.

COME ON, THEN.

AH, I SEE...

H-HEY. ARE YOU REALLY A...

NICE!

BUT HOW? AREN'T YOU GUYS SUPPOSED TO BE IMMORTAL?

THE POPULATION HERE DROPS?

YEAH. AND IT TOOK ME, LIKE, ALL OF 30 SECONDS TO FIND A BROKER ON THE 'NET WILLING TO KICK THIS WHOLE THING OFF. DIRT CHEAP, TOO.

Y'KNOW, THIS WAS ALL PRETTY EASY... ALMOST TOO EASY. I MEAN, NOBODY ON THE TOUR EVEN BOTHERED LOOKING FOR US.

YOU'LL FIND OUT SOON ENOUGH.

C'MON.

BUT, WELL, THE BUND'S POPULATION DOES NOTHING BUT GO STRAIGHT DOWN, SO THAT LAW AIN'T EXACTLY ALL THAT STRICTLY ENFORCED.

GENERALLY IS. TECHNICALLY, THIS ALL'S ILLEGAL...

COOL ...!

THIS PLACE IS... TOTALLY DIFFERENT FROM WHAT WE SAW IN THE AFTER-NOON!

QUIT STARING AROUND LIKE A BUNCH OF HICKS, AND STICK WITH ME, OKAY? IF EITHER OF YOU GETS BIT OUT HERE, I DON'T GET PAID.

BACK OFF, BABE.

THESE TWO AIN'T FOOD. THEY'VE GOT SOMEBODY WHO WANTS TO MEET THEM.

W H O A !

YEAH. THE GUY WHO'S GOING TO TURN YOU INTO VAMPIRES.

OUR "MASTER"?

YOUR NEW MASTER IS WAITING INSIDE.

HERE IT IS.

HEH HEH... WELL, THIS IS IT.

SO YEAH, I STABBED THAT "SERPIENTES" GUY. BUT GUESS WHAT? I USED THAT KNIFE!

WHAT?!

YOUR KNIFE!

DUDE, LET'S NOT DO THIS! WE SHOULD GO BACK.

WHAT, NOW?!

OI!

THERE'S STILL TIME! WE CAN GO HOME, AND--

WE CAN'T GO HOME, MAN! ME OR YOU!

DEAL WITH IT. YOU AIN'T GOT NO CHOICE.

RRG...

YOU BAS-TARD !!

YOU GO BACK, AND YOU'LL GO DOWN FOR MURDER, MAN!!

I GOT YOU HERE, SO MY JOB'S DONE.

YOU TWO DONE NOW? GOOD. GO IN.

HUH? WHAT?

HAH HAH HAH

DID I SAY SOME-THING FUNNY?

ARE YOU THE GUY WHO'S GOING TO TURN ME INTO A VAMPIRE?

HE WAS ASKING WHICH ONE OF YOU WANTS TO GO FIRST.

C'MON, SPEAK JAPANESE!!

I CAN'T UNDERSTAND A WORD YOU'RE SAYING!

WHOA, HOLD IT! I'M NOT HERE FOR THAT! I'M JUST ALONG FOR THE RIDE!!

SLEAZY BASTARD...

THE BROKER SAID THERE WOULD BE TWO. WE PAID FOR TWO.

HEY, WHERE ARE YOU GOING?!

DAM-MIT!

NOW THAT I'M A VAMPIRE, I CAN DO WHATEVER THE HELL I WANT.

REALLY... Y'KNOW, I THINK I'LL GO HOME TOO.

I'VE HAD ENOUGH OF THIS!!

HOME...

TCH!

FREEZE!!

FASH

FSHHH

OW! THAT'S HOT!

WHA...

WE'RE TOURISTS FROM THE MAINLAND! WE'RE JUST TRYING TO GO HOME!

HUH? WHAT'RE YOU TALKING ABOUT?

THIS IS YOUR FIRST WARNING! YOU ARE APPROACHING THE UNDERSEA TUNNEL WITHOUT PERMISSION.

TURN BACK IMMEDIATELY.

ALL THOSE INFECTED ARE FORBIDDEN TO LEAVE THE ISLAND.

YOU ARE INFECTED WITH THE VAMPIRISM VIRUS.

SHUT UP!

MASAKI, IF YOU HADN'T-- RRGH!!

ALL RIGHT, SO WE CAN'T GO BACK. SO WHAT?

LET'S MAKE NEW LIVES FOR OURSELVES AS VAMPIRES. THAT'LL BE LOADS MORE FUN, ANYWAY!

RIGHT, RIGHT.

IT'S ALL MY FAULT. AGAIN.

DAM- MIT.

I SHOULD'VE JUST LEFT YOU ALONE.

YOU TWO.

BRRM

PSHHHH

I DIDN'T HEAR ANYTHING ABOUT A SHIPMENT COMING IN TODAY...

THUK

IT'S THE VGS!! THEY'RE ON TO US!

!

BRAT-TAT

BRRM

BRAT-TAT-TAT

WHOA!

BLAM

BLAM

BLAM

I CAN'T BELIEVE THEY'RE ACTUALLY...

THEY'RE NUTS!

WHAT THE HELL ARE THEY DOING?!

YOU TWO. YOU GO OUT TOO.

GRAB

GYAH!

HEY!

WHAT THE HELL IS GOING ON? I DON'T GET ANY OF THIS...

......

WHAT... THE HELL WAS ALL THAT?

HUH? WHY?

LET'S GO BACK TO THAT FIRST BAR.

SO YOU THINK HE'LL TELL US SOME-THING...? FEH!

AND I BET YOU WANT US TO WALK ALL THE WAY BACK THERE TOO, DAMMIT.

SO DOESN'T THAT MEAN MR. TATTOO IS THE GUY WHO PLANNED THIS WHOLE HEIST?

THAT GUY WHO BLEW HIMSELF UP, OUR "MASTER" OR WHATEVER...

IT LOOKED LIKE HE WAS SOME SORT OF LACKEY TO THAT GUY WITH THE TRIBAL TATTOOS.

WHAT'S THIS STUFF ...?

SAND?

NO, ASH. HOW'D IT GET IN HERE?

WHAT HAPPENED HERE?

WAIT... THOSE ARE CORPSES.

VAMPIRE CORPSES.

BY... SOMEBODY.

THEY MUST'VE BEEN ATTACKED ...

BLEAH!!

FWUE

WHAT THE HELL IS GOING ON HERE?!

ATTACKED, AND SLAUGHTERED!

OH MY GOD...

WMP

HEISTS, BOMBS, SUICIDAL MANIACS, AND TOTAL MASSACRES!

WAH?!

THMP

THESE VAMPIRES ARE INSANE! COMPLETELY, FREAKIN' INSANE!!

WHAT THE --?!

THMP

THMP

Chapter 3: The Underground Kingdom

ARE YOU OKAY?

I'VE GOT TO CHECK. DO YOU MIND?

WHY WERE YOU STUFFED INTO THAT SUITCASE?

THEN... I WAS HERE...

I.... I WAS KIDNAPPED. I REMEMBER GETTING GRABBED AS I CAME OUT OF WORK.

DUH, THEY'RE ALL OVER. JUST GRAB SOME OUT OF THOSE ASH PILES.

WHERE? I DON'T HAVE ANY...

HEY, AKIRA.

GO GET THE GIRL SOME CLOTHES, WOULD YOU?

NH ...

YOU TOO, HUH?

ALL RIGHT... I'LL BE BACK IN A SEC.

KYAAA!!

SO, THIS IS WHAT IT LOOKS LIKE WHEN VAMPIRES DIE...

GOD...

FWUP

EEK!

WHAT'S WRONG WITH THAT? THE GIRL'S ALREADY BEEN BIT ONCE.

SO I WANTED TO TRY SUCKIN' A LITTLE BLOOD, OKAY?

WHAT, WASN'T IT OBVIOUS? WE'RE VAMPIRES NOW, MAN.

OW...

LET'S GIVE IT A TRY.

HEEEY... THAT MEANS SHE'S A VAMP NOW TOO, RIGHT? I WONDER WHAT HAPPENS IF A VAMPIRE SUCKS ANOTHER VAMPIRE'S BLOOD?

YEAH, YEAH. WHAT-EVER.

EVERY-THING'S MY FAULT. EVERY-THING'S ALWAYS MY FAULT.

AND THANKS TO YOU, MY WHOLE LIFE HAS BEEN--

I NEVER SHOULD'VE COME HERE WITH YOU!

SCREW IT. I'VE HAD ENOUGH.

I AM SO OUT OF HERE!

NOT USING IT WOULD BE A TOTAL CRIME!

WE'VE GOT POWER NOW, MAN! SUPER-HUMAN POWER!

HA... HA HA!

......

MAN, DID YOU SEE THAT?!

KYAA!

SLAM

I'M NOT SURPRISED YOU DON'T WANT TO. YOU'VE ALWAYS BEEN A FREAKIN' COWARD!

SO STAY HERE, MAN! STAY CURLED UP IN YOUR LITTLE HOLE, DRINKING BLOOD OUT OF WHATEVER RATS YOU CAN CATCH!

......

SORRY. I HOPE WE DIDN'T SCARE YOU TOO MUCH.

SO, UH... IT LOOKS LIKE IT'S ALMOST TIME FOR SUNUP.

HERE.

I DUSTED IT OFF AS BEST I COULD, BUT IT'S STILL PRETTY ASHY. GROSS, I KNOW.

THEN AGAIN, THERE'S NO GUARANTEES THAT WHOEVER DID ALL THIS WON'T BE COMING BACK...

GETTING HIT BY SUNLIGHT ISN'T SUPPOSED TO BE VERY GOOD FOR VAMPIRES, SO I GUESS IT'S PROBABLY SMART FOR US TO STAY HERE...

ALL RIGHT...

THIS PLACE... I DON'T LIKE IT.

I DON'T WANT TO STAY.

LET'S LOOK FOR SOME PLACE OUT OF THE SUN.

NOW! HURRY!

VAMPIRES HERE USUALLY HANG OUT UNDERGROUND DURING DAYLIGHT HOURS.

BUT EVERY NOW AND AGAIN, WE GET A NEWBIE WHO DOESN'T MAKE IT IN TIME AND GETS STUCK OUT HERE WHEN THE SUN'S COMING UP.

FSHT

AH... SO YOU'RE NEW, HUH?

I GUESS THAT MAKES SENSE.

ME? NOPE.

SO, UM... YOU'RE NOT A VAMPIRE?

VWMM

VWMM

FSHH

UM... I DON'T THINK I'D QUALIFY AS "NORMAL."

THEN WHAT'S A NORMAL HUMAN DOING HERE?

AH, I SEE... SO THAT'S YOUR SITUATION, HUH.

UH, I DON'T EXACTLY, UM...

.....

YOU CAN'T DO ANYTHING IN THIS PLACE WITHOUT GETTING REGISTERED FIRST.

WHY DON'T I TAKE YOU OVER TO THE BUND'S IMMIGRATION OFFICE?

SO WHERE'S THE APARTMENT YOU WERE GIVEN? I'LL WALK YOU THERE.

TO YOU, WHO RESIDE IN MY LAND, I SWEAR TO PROTECT AND NURTURE YOU TO THE UTMOST OF MY ABILITY, WITH BOUNDLESS LOVE AND RESPECT.

WELCOME, MY BELOVED CHILDREN OF THE NIGHT.

NO...

HERE. FILL OUT YOUR NAME ON HERE.

DO YOU HAVE ANY PERSONAL ID FROM THE OUTSIDE?

AH. OH WELL.

SHE'S VERY CUTE.

AS LONG AS YOU REMAIN...

ON THE OUTSIDE, MAYBE.

SO THAT'S THE VAMPIRE QUEEN, HUH?

HEY, YOUR NAME IS "AKIRA"?

HUH?

name:名前

Akira

ISN'T IT?

REALLY? THAT IS KINDA NEAT.

MY NAME'S "AKIRA," TOO.

NEAT.

AND AS A CITIZEN, THE GOVERNMENT WILL PROVIDE YOU WITH HOUSING AND FOOD AT NO COST TO YOU.

ANYWAY, ALL THAT'S LEFT IS TO HAVE ONE OF THE RECEPTIONISTS HERE PROCESS YOUR APPLICATION, AND *VOILA!* YOU'RE OFFICIALLY A CITIZEN OF THE BLUND.

UH, NO... IT'S BRAZIL.

I ASSUME YOUR COUNTRY OF ORIGIN IS JAPAN?

AKIRA GARCIA FUJISAKI-SAN, YES?

MAN, WHO WOULD'VE GUESSED THAT BECOMING A VAMPIRE WOULD BE THIS... BUREAU-CRATIC.

DO YOU HAVE ANY RELATIVES YOU WOULD LIKE TO NOTIFY OF YOUR ACCEPTANCE TO THE BLUND?

ONE...

NO, MA'AM.

DO YOU HAVE ANY BLOOD-BORNE OR INHERITED MEDICAL CONDITIONS THAT WE SHOULD BE AWARE OF?

I'LL NEVER BE ABLE TO GO BACK AGAIN.

FOREVER...

THEN THAT'S IT. I'M A VAMPIRE. MY OLD LIFE WILL BE GONE.

ONCE THIS DRY, STERILE EXCHANGE OF INFOR-MATION IS FINISHED...

HM? LEMME SEE.

IS THIS OKAY ...?

HOLD IT!!!

GOD...

WHY DIDN'T YOU TELL ME THAT SOONER?!

WHY?

UM... YESTERDAY? SOMETIME AROUND... UH... EIGHT OR SO? I THINK?

WHEN DID YOU TWO GET BITTEN? HOW LONG AGO?!

Chapter 4: The Queen & Me

WOULD YOU?

WAIT, HUH...?

RIGHT.

EXACTLY.

HM?

HOLD IT. YOU DON'T HAVE TO COME ALL THE WAY OVER HERE YOURSELF...

UH, OKAY...

WELL, I'LL SEE YOU WHEN YOU GET HERE, THEN.

VAMPIRISM IS, AT ITS ROOT, A VIRUS. IT SPREADS AND GROWS JUST LIKE ANY OTHER VIRUS DOES.

SORRY ABOUT THAT.

SNAP

ANYWAY, BACK TO WHAT I WAS SAYING BEFORE...

MORE SPECIFICALLY, IT'S A TYPE OF *RETRO-VIRUS*. IT LATCHES ON TO YOUR DNA AND REWRITES IT, TURNING YOU FROM A NORMAL HUMAN INTO SOMETHING COMPLETELY DIFFERENT.

SO THERE'S A VIRUS INSIDE ME, CHANGING MY DNA...?

DON'T WORRY. JUST LIKE MANY OTHER VIRUSES, THERE'S A VACCINE.

WITH THE PROPER DOSE, THE VIRUS'S PROGRESS CAN BE REVERSED, RETURNING YOU TO A NORMAL HUMAN.

WE CAN REALLY GO BACK TO BEING HUMAN?!

WE CAN GO BACK...?

A VAMPIRE *VACCINE*? THERE IS SUCH A THING?!

THREE DAYS?

GREAT! THAT'S PLENTY OF TIME.

YOU TWO ARE *INCREDIBLY LUCKY* THAT WE FOUND YOU.

JUST ONE THING, THOUGH. THERE'S A TIME LIMIT.

IT TAKES SOMEWHERE AROUND 72 HOURS TO GO FROM FIRST BITE TO FULL-ON VAMPIRISM.

ABOVE THAT, THE VIRUS HAS GENERALLY PROGRESSED TOO FAR FOR THE VACCINE TO FIX.

ACTUALLY, YOU'RE LOOKING AT CLOSER TO 48 HOURS IF YOU WANT TO BE REVERSED.

SO ONLY ABOUT 30 HOURS...

14:00

YOU WERE BITTEN AT 8 PM. AND IT'S 2 PM NOW.

REALLY?

OH, THANK GOD!

DEFINITELY. YOU TWO SHOULD BE ABLE TO GO HOME COMPLETELY HUMAN TODAY.

BUT THAT IS STILL PLENTY OF TIME, RIGHT?

YEAH. THANK GOD.

I CAN GO BACK...

I...

AKIRA.

HERE IS FINE. I ASKED A FRIEND TO GO GRAB SOME FOR YOU.

SHE SHOULD BE HERE ANY MINUTE NOW...

SO WHERE DO WE HAVE TO GO TO GET THIS VACCINE?

IT'S, UH, KIND OF A LONG STORY.

UH, I GUESS YOU COULD SAY THAT, YEAH. HOW TO EXPLAIN THIS...

OH MY GOSH! WHO ARE YOU?!

OH, IT'S ALL RIGHT, EVERYONE. GO BACK TO WORK.

SO THE "FRIEND" YOU ASKED TO "GO GRAB SOME" WAS THE QUEEN?!

I WANT YOU TO LISTEN TO ME CALMLY, UNDER-STAND?

ABOUT THAT...

ANYWAY, HIME-SAN, DID YOU BRING THE VACCINE?

WAIT, WHAT THE HELL? WE SHOULD HAVE TONS OF THAT STUFF STOCKPILED AT EVERY MEDICAL FACILITY IN THE BUND!

HUH ...?!

WE HAVE NO VACCINE.

THE VACCINE WE KEPT AT OUR MEDICAL FACILITIES WAS RECENTLY DISCOVERED TO BE CONTAMINATED, RENDERING ALL OF IT UNUSABLE.

IT APPEARS SOME FOREIGN PARTICLES GOT INTO IT SOMEWHERE IN THE PRODUCTION PROCESS.

I HAD TO HAVE THE ENTIRE PRODUCTION LINE SHUT DOWN UNTIL THE CAUSE OF THE CONTAMINANT IS FOUND.

OH NO...

THEN CAN'T WE JUST USE THAT STUFF?

IMMEDIATELY AFTER I FIRST HEARD OF THIS PROBLEM, I ORDERED SOME OF OUR EMERGENCY SUPPLY SHIPPED IN FROM OVERSEAS...

LAST NIGHT, AN UNKNOWN GROUP OF THIEVES STOLE INTO THE WAREHOUSE IN WHICH IT WAS STORED AND **BLEW IT UP--** TRUCK, CONTAINER, BUILDING, AND ALL.

NO. THAT SUPPLY IS NOW GONE, AS WELL.

SO YOU WERE ONE OF THE PERPE-TRATORS INVOLVED.

I SEE...

WHAT HAVE I DONE ...?!

HN.

?

DO YOU RECALL THE ONE WHO ORDERED YOU TO ASSIST THEM?

··········

VERA.

I... I'M SORRY, YOUR MAJ-ESTY... I DON'T.

I NEVER GOT HIS NAME. BESIDES, HE BLEW HIMSELF UP, ALONG WITH EVERYBODY ELSE.

HAVE BEOWULF SEARCH THE BAR THIS BOY WAS FIRST TAKEN TO.

THERE MAY BE SOME CLUES.

OH, VERA-SAN. DIDN'T SEE YOU THERE.

YES, YOUR MAJ-ESTY.

TOK

YES, YOUR MAJ-ESTY.

......

HE WAS PART OF THE GANG THAT DID IT.

WHAT'RE YOU GOING TO DO WITH HIM?

HIME-SAN...

THE LOWER-RANKED VAMPIRE HAS NO CHOICE. THEY MUST ABSOLUTELY OBEY THE ORDERS OF THEIR SUPERIOR. WAS THAT NOT THE CASE FOR YOU?

HUH...?

DO NOT WORRY.

IT FELT ALMOST LIKE HE'D HYPNOTIZED ME, OR SOMETHING.

WRONG ANSWER.

YEAH...

YOU ARE ALLOWED BUT ONE THING TO SAY. "YES, MASTER."

A LOWER-RANKED VAMPIRE IS NOT PUNISHED FOR COMMITTING A CRIME THAT A HIGHER-RANKED VAMPIRE ORDERED THEM TO DO.

THIS IS MUCH THE SAME THING.

NOT THE GUN HE HAD USED.

WHEN A PERSON COMMITS A CRIME, IT IS HE WHO IS PUNISHED.

HOWEVER, I'M AFRAID THAT DOES NOT MEAN THE BURDEN THAT THOSE ACTS HAVE PLACED UPON YOUR SHOULDERS WILL DISAPPEAR JUST AS EASILY.

SO, SO SORRY.

I'M SORRY...

THEY'LL NEVER NOTICE...

WHAT? IT'S JUST A SOUVENIR.

WHAT, ME?

WHAT ARE YOU STANDING AROUND FOR?

WHEN A LADY CRIES, YOU OFFER HER A HANDKERCHIEF!

WHAT?!

WAIT!

THERE'S STILL SOME VACCINE LEFT!!

I DON'T KNOW HOW MANY HE GRABBED, BUT I SAW HIM SHOVE THEM IN HIS POCKET!

MY FRIEND SWIPED SOME WHEN NO ONE ELSE WAS LOOKING!

I DON'T KNOW... ER, YOUR MAJESTY. BUT IF WE CAN FIND HIM...

WHERE IS YOUR FRIEND NOW?

WE CAN GO BACK TO BEING HUMAN AGAIN.

OF COURSE! THIS IS DIRECTLY CONNECTED TO AN INCIDENT OF GREAT IMPORTANCE TO MY BUND!

WHAT, YOU'RE COMING TOO?

LET US FIND THIS FRIEND OF YOURS!

SMAK

EXCELLENT! THEN IT IS DECIDED!

IT SEEMS THIS CASE HAS MORE TO IT THAN IT SEEMS.

BESIDES...

WHERE DO YOU WANT US TO START LOOKING?

!

BOY! DESCRIBE TO MY SECRETARY WHAT THIS FRIEND OF YOURS LOOKS LIKE.

WE WILL SEARCH FOR HIM USING THE BUND'S SECURITY CAMERAS.

BESIDES, I CAN HARDLY LET YOU DO THIS ALONE, AFTER HEARING WHAT YOU'VE BEEN THROUGH.

YEAH. HIME-SAN'S ALL GUNG-HO ABOUT IT.

YOU'RE GOING TO HELP US?

THANKS...

HE IS SOMETHING OF A "HEAD PRISONER" TO THE OTHER CITIZENS.

HE MAY KNOW WHERE WE CAN FIND THIS FRIEND OF YOURS.

WHEN SOMEONE FIRST COMES HERE, THEY FIND THEIR WAY TO HIM SOONER OR LATER, WHETHER THEY ARRIVED LEGALLY OR NOT.

FIRST, THERE IS SOMEONE WE MUST MEET.

WHO?

MY BUND IS A LABYRINTH. THERE IS NO TIME TO LOSE!

WE HAVE ONLY 30 HOURS!

TOK

TOK

I, UH, NEVER DID GET YOUR NAME.

UM... Y'KNOW?

·······

RULI.

C'MON, RULI.

WE WILL FIND A WAY TO BE HUMAN AGAIN.

I PROMISE YOU...

Chapter 5: The Child

HARVEY.

WELL, WELL ...

OKAY, EVERY- BODY... OUT.

WHAT THE --?!

A LITTLE BABY?

A GOOD EVENIN' TO YA, YER MAJESTY.

WHAT BUSINESS BRINGS YER ROYAL TOOSH DOWN HERE TO MY HUMBLE HOLE?

ANYWAY, WHAT BUSINESS BRINGS YER ROY-ALNESS DOWN HERE?

YOU DIDN'T COME HERE JUST TO POKE AT MY REPUTATION, I'M SURE.

OUCH. YOU WOUND ME, YER MAJESTY.

DO NOT LET HIS LOOKS FOOL YOU. HE MAY LOOK LIKE A SWEET, INNOCENT CHILD, BUT IN ACTUALITY, HE IS OVER A HUNDRED YEARS OLD, AND AS SLY AS THEY COME. NOT TO MENTION, HE IS QUITE TWISTED.

YES. EVERYONE, THIS IS HARVEY, THE UNOFFICIAL CARETAKER OF MY BUND'S RESIDENTS.

SO THAT'S WHAT WAS GOIN' ON BEHIND THAT EXPLOSION...

A-HA. I SEE...

MEBBIE YOUR KID GOT TAKEN IN BY ONE OF THOSE "SOME-BODIES."

RUMOR IS, THOUGH, SOMEBODY'S TAKIN' THEM IN AND MAKIN' THEM DO SOME PRETTY SHADY STUFF.

WELL, I WISH I COULD TELL YA THAT I'VE SEEN THE KID, BUT HE HASN'T BEEN THROUGH HERE YET.

GOT WAY TOO MANY COMIN' IN BY ROUTES THAT AIN'T EXACTLY LEGIT THESE DAYS. RIFFRAFF LIKE THAT, THEY DON'T GIVE TWO DAMNS ABOUT DUTY AN' PROPER COURTESY.

NOW THAT'S AN ODD QUES-TION.

ANYBODY ON THIS ISLAND ONLY EVER DOES STUFF FOR ONE REASON...

"FOR YER MAJESTY'S SAKE." ANYBODY PLOTTIN' AND PLANNIN' AROUND HERE AIN'T DOIN' IT AGAINST YER MAJESTY, THAT'S FOR DAMN SURE.

FOR HER MAJESTY...

!

REALLY, NOW... THIS IS THE FIRST I'VE HEARD OF THAT.

WHO ARE THESE MISCRE-ANTS? WHAT ARE THEY PLOTTING, AND WHY?

THEN DO SO.

THAT, YER MAJESTY, I COULDN'T TELL YA. I'M JUST AS MYSTIFIED.

PROLLY THE ONLY WAY TO FIND OUT WOULD BE TO NAB ONE OF 'EM AND ASK.

HOW IS DESTROYING MY OWN VACCINE FOR MY SAKE?

UM, E-EXCUSE ME...?

HN?

PHONE!

AS YA WISH, THEN. HAVE A SIT OUTSIDE, IF YA WOULDN'T MIND.

I'LL HAVE SOME OF MY BOYS START NOSIN' AROUND FOR THAT KID.

WE'RE GOING TO BE STUCK LIVING AS VAMPIRES, RIGHT?

IF WE CAN'T FIND THE VACCINE IN TIME...

HOW IS IT DIFFERENT FROM LIVING AS A HUMAN?

WHAT'S IT LIKE? LIVING AS A VAMPIRE.

GETTIN' TURNED CAN BE GOOD OR BAD. JUST DEPENDS ON WHO YOU ASK.

I CAN TELL YOU THIS, THOUGH.

SEE, IN *MY* CASE, MY MA WENT AND CHOMPED DOWN ON ME ALMOST RIGHT AFTER THEY CUT THE UMBILICAL CORD.

I'VE BEEN A VAMPIRE FOR AS LONG AS I CAN REMEMBER. AIN'T GOT NO HUMAN MEMORIES TO BEGIN WITH.

HN. WELL, AIN'T THAT A DOOZY OF A QUESTION ...

YOU ASKIN' ME THAT? OR JUST IN GENERAL?

DOESN'T MATTER HOW OLD I GET, I'LL NEVER BE ABLE TO GET AROUND ON MY OWN WITHOUT A WALKER.

AND NEVER MIND FANGS... I DON'T EVEN GOT ALL OF MY MILK TEETH IN YET!

BUT OTHERS, WELL, THEY AIN'T AS LUCKY.

TAKE A LOOK AT ME.

YOU, BABE, *YOU* COULD PROLLY LIVE IT UP.

TRUST ME, BEIN' A HUNDRED-YEAR-OLD VIRGIN AIN'T NO LAUGHIN' MATTER.

HEH. DON'T GOT ANY HAIR *DOWN THERE* YET, EITHER.

YOU'RE YOUNG, SEXY, AND IN PERFECT HEALTH. GUYS LIKE THAT, THEY CAN REALLY GET THE MOST OUTTA BEIN' A VAMPIRE.

PAT

THREE DAYS, AN' I'LL TEACH YA EVERY-THING THERE IS--BOTH ABOVE BOARD, AND BELOW.

AH WELL. IF THERE'S EVER ANYTHIN' YOU WANNA KNOW ABOUT VAMPIRES, BABE, COME SEE ME.

....

AS FOR THE CHOICE BETWEEN HUMAN OR VAMPIRE... ALL LIVING THINGS HAVE WITHIN THEMSELVES AN AFFLICTION, SHALL WE CALL IT?

YOU TWO HAVE ALREADY DECIDED TO REGAIN YOUR HUMANITY.

HEH.

THAT WAS UNNECESSARY, I'M SURE. MY APOLOGIES.

A CHRONIC AFFLICTION, ABOUT WHICH NOTHING CAN BE DONE. PERHAPS IT IS THAT WHICH DIVIDES WHO CHOOSES HUMANITY, AND WHO CHOOSES VAMPIRISM.

DID SOMETHING HAPPEN?!

SORRY, AKIRA. IT APPEARS I MUST RETURN TO MY OFFICE IMMEDIATELY.

YES...?

AH. I SEE.

YOUR MAJESTY. A CALL FROM WOLFGANG-DONO.

YES. IT HAS BEEN DETERMINED THAT THE CONTAMINANT FOUND IN THE VACCINE WE PRODUCED WAS INTRODUCED INTENTION- ALLY.

SOME- ONE'S SABO- TAGING OUR VACCINE PRO- DUC- TION?!

YES. IT SEEMS THE ROOTS OF THIS LITTLE INCIDENT RUN *FAR DEEPER* THAN I EXPECTED.

ESPE- CIALLY YOUR NAME.

IT IS NOT A PROB- LEM. I HAVE TAKEN A LIKING TO YOU, YOU KNOW.

ER, THANKS, YOUR MAJESTY ...

I AM GOING TO INVESTIGATE THIS FROM A DIFFERENT ANGLE. DON'T WORRY. WE WILL SOLVE THIS YET.

. . . .

I GET EVERYDAY WORDS JUST FINE, BUT A LOT OF THE MORE COMPLEX JAPANESE WORDS OUT THERE ARE STILL BEYOND ME.

I LIVED IN BRAZIL UNTIL I WAS SEVEN, SO JAPANESE ISN'T MY FIRST LANGUAGE.

UM, HEY.

HUH?

WHAT DID HIME-SAMA MEAN WHEN SHE SAID "AFFLICTION"?

MY... DESTINY...

DESTINY, HUH...

ALTHOUGH, IN THIS CASE, I THINK HIME-SAN WAS MEANING IT MORE LIKE A DESTINY THAT EVERYONE'S BORN WITH.

"AFFLICTION" GENERALLY MEANS SOME KIND OF ILLNESS OR ANOTHER.

YOU SAID YOU'RE FROM BRAZIL? SO YOU'RE JAPANESE-BRAZILIAN?

HEY.

YOU CAN TELL?

YOU'RE ONLY HALF TOO, RIGHT?

YEAH. SOME- HOW, YOU JUST LOOK IT.

YEAH. MY FAMILY IMMI- GRATED THERE A WHILE AGO. I'M... FOURTH GEN, I THINK.

MY MOM IS PURE BRAZILIAN, SO I'M REALLY ONLY HALF JAPANESE.

YOU LOOK KINDA CAUCASIAN.

SO WHERE'S YOUR DAD FROM? EUROPE? AMERICA?

IN MY CASE, MY MOM IS THE ONE WHO'S JAPANESE.

YEAH. THE ECONOMY OVER IN BRAZIL WASN'T DOING ALL THAT HOT WHEN I WAS LITTLE.

SO A LOT OF BRAZILIANS AND JAPANESE- BRAZILIANS CAME OVER HERE TO TRY AND MAKE A BETTER LIVING, AND TO SEND MONEY BACK TO THEIR FAMILIES IN BRAZIL. MINE WAS ONE OF THOSE.

DID THE REST OF YOUR FAMILY COME BACK TO JAPAN WITH YOU?

WELL, THAT'S KINDA HARD TO EXPLAIN ...

UM...

FINDING HIM WAS EASY.

LUCKY FOR US, THAT FRIEND OF YOURS IS A GRAND-SLAM CLASS BONEHEAD.

SORRY FOR THE WAIT, KIDS.

WHAT'S THAT SUP-POSED TO MEAN?

YES, THAT IS VERY STUPID.

THAT IDIOT.

TOOK ALL OF TWO SECONDS TO FIND HIM.

THE KID'S WANDERING AROUND THE ROUGHER STREETS, SHOWING THOSE AMPULES TO ANYBODY HE CAN GRAB.

ALL JUST SO HE CAN FIND OUT WHAT'S WRITTEN ON 'EM.

WHAT?!

SEEMS SOMEBODY GOT TO HIM BEFORE US. HE WAS NABBED AND DRAGGED OFF. DUNNO WHERE.

THAT'S THE PROBLEM.

SO WHERE IS HE, THEN?

LIKE I SAID, I DUNNO.

HOW-EVER...

WHO WOULD'VE DONE SOME-THING LIKE THAT?

WHERE COULD THEY HAVE TAKEN HIM?

REALLY? THAT'S GREAT NEWS!

GOTH-WHA...?

WHAT'S THAT?

AND ALL OF 'EM WAS DECKED OUT IN THE LATEST GOTH-LOLI FASHION.

I DO KNOW THE ONES DOIN' THE GRABBIN' WERE A BUNCH OF YOUNG CHICKS.

HEY ...

LOOKS LIKE THE SUN'S TOTALLY SET.

THERE'S ONLY ONE GUY WHO WOULD DO SOMETHING LIKE THAT, AND I KNOW *EXACTLY* WHO HE IS.

NAH, WE DON'T NEED TO. SEE, HE'S COMING TO US.

ARE YOU *SURE* WE SHOULDN'T BE GOING AFTER THE GUY WHO GRABBED MASAKI?

BRUUUM

THE LAST THING I EXPECTED WAS A CALL FROM YOU.

WELL, WILL THE WONDERS NEVER CEASE?

Chapter 6: Night on the Planet

HIS SPECIALTY IS DOING THE DIRTY WORK.

HE MAY NOT LOOK IT, BUT HE'S ONE OF THE HIGHER-RANKING NOBLES SERVING THE TEPES ROYAL FAMILY.

BUT PLEASE, CALL ME AL-PHONSE.

ALPHONSE MEDICI BORGIANI.

VAMPIRE NOBILITY ...?

WE'VE GOT BUSINESS WITH THAT GUY, BY THE WAY. I WANT TO SEE HIM.

SO HAVING A PACK OF YOUR GOTH-LOLI GROUPIES NAB A RANDOM GUY OFF THE STREET IS A MATTER OF NATIONAL SECURITY?

HEY NOW. DON'T BE RUDE.

MY OFFICIAL RESPONSIBILITIES ARE THE SECURITY OF THE ROYAL FAMILY, AND DIRECTING COUNTER-INTELLIGENCE OPERATIONS.

WE NEED TO QUESTION HIM *THOROUGHLY* ABOUT WHO WAS BEHIND IT AND WHAT THEY WERE AFTER.

HE'S A SURVIVOR OF THE TERROR- IST GROUP THAT BLEW UP A ROYAL WARE- HOUSE.

WHY ?!

CAN'T DO THAT, I'M AFRAID.

IT LOOKS LIKE YOU AND I ARE GOING TO HAVE TO HAVE A TALK, KID. COME WITH ME.

WHA ...?

REALLY NOW?

HEY!

HE WON'T KNOW! NEITHER OF US KNEW! WE WERE JUST BROUGHT HERE AND ORDERED TO DO IT! WE DIDN'T HAVE A CHOICE!!

HE WAS THERE TOO. SAYS HE'S A FRIEND OF THE ONE YOU GOT.

HE'S BEEN GIVEN FULL IMMUNITY AND PERMISSION TO GO WHERE HE WILL.

HIME-SAN HAS HIM UNDER HER PERSONAL PROTECTION.

I JUST SAID I DON'T KNOW ANYTHING!!

CALM DOWN.

HER MAJESTY CAN BE ENTIRELY *TOO* FORGIVING OF HER LOWEST SUBJECTS.

SHEESH.

HE MANAGED TO ESCAPE.

I DON'T HAVE HIM.

WE'RE JUST LOOKING FOR THE LAST OF THE VACCINE HE'S CARRYING.

LISTEN, WE'RE NOT TRYING TO STEP ON YOUR TOES HERE. YOU CAN KEEP THE GUY.

WHAT? *WHY*?!

AFRAID I CAN'T DO THAT, EITHER.

HE'S A SLIPPERY ONE, THAT KID.

MY PEOPLE WERE ATTACKED BY AN UNKNOWN GROUP WHILE THEY WERE BRINGING HIM IN.

HE GOT LOOSE AND DISAPPEARED DURING THE SCUFFLE.

SERIOUSLY?!

MASAKI...

DAMMIT! NOT AGAIN!

THERE WERE PROBABLY MORE PEOPLE INVOLVED THAN WHAT YOU THINK.

BUT... EVERYONE THAT DIDN'T GET BLOWN UP GOT STAKED AT THE BAR...

REMNANTS OF THE GROUP THAT BLEW THE WAREHOUSE, MOST LIKELY.

WHAT ABOUT THE GROUP THAT ATTACKED YOU?

THIS ORGANIZATION COULD BE MUCH LARGER THAN WHAT ANY OF US REALIZED.

IT SEEMS THE ROOTS OF THIS LITTLE INCIDENT RUN FAR DEEPER THAN WHAT I EXPECTED.

THIS IS WHERE WE LOST HIM...

WE'RE CONDUCTING A SEARCH OURSELVES.

YOU SURE YOU'RE OKAY WITH JUST LETTING US GO?

YOU'RE GOING TO GO ON LOOKING FOR HIM, RIGHT?

THE MORE PEOPLE WE HAVE ON THIS, THE BETTER.

BUT WE ALSO HAVE TO SEND PEOPLE TO INVESTIGATE THE SABOTAGE AT THE VACCINE PRODUCTION PLANT.

AL-PHONSE.

AND KEEP AN EYE ON US FOR YOU, RIGHT?

HEH.

SHE'LL TAKE YOU TO THE EXACT SPOT WHERE HE GOT AWAY.

YOU CAN'T BE TOO CAREFUL AROUND THEM.

WATCH YOURSELVES OUT THERE. THIS AREA IS WHERE IMMIGRANTS FROM THE OTHER CLANS USUALLY WIND UP.

OKAY...

LET'S GET GOING.

BUT I CAN'T SAY I'VE EVER BEEN IN THIS PART.

I'VE BEEN IN THE BUND ALMOST SINCE IT WAS FIRST COMPLETED...

THE SILENT TYPE, HUH?

HEY, ARE WE THERE YET?

GOD. THIS PLACE IS PRACTICALLY A FAVELA*...

*Favela = Brazilian-Portuguese for "slum."

IT'S DEAD QUIET. EVERYBODY JUST VANISHED...

!

HERE THEY COME!

GOD, ARE YOU OKAY?

Chapter 7: Human Farm

THEN ALL THIS PENT-UP EMOTION STARTED COMING OUT. I COULDN'T STOP.

SORRY. I... I GUESS I JUST SNAPPED.

LETTING YOUR EMOTIONS GET OUT OF CONTROL, AND DOING GOD KNOWS WHAT CRAZY STUFF...

GUYS LIKE YOU, YOU'RE THE *WORST* TYPE TO GET TURNED.

THAT'S THE NUMBER ONE CAUSE OF DEATH FOR VAMPIRES.

HUH?

YEAH, IT LOOKS LIKE YOU NEED TO GET REVERSED BACK TO HUMAN, NO MATTER WHAT.

!

THE BLIND'S POPULATION DOES NOTHING BUT GO STRAIGHT DOWN...

SQUEEZE

....

THERE YOU ARE! WHERE THE HELL DID YOU DISAPPEAR TO, RIGHT WHEN WE NEEDED YOU?!

I FOLLOWED THE ONES WHO RAN. I KNEW YOU WOULD BE ABLE TO HANDLE THE REST.

EVEN HER HUMMING IS SPECIAL.

I KNEW SHE WAS RULI.

WELL, THANKS FOR THE COMPLIMENT, BUT STILL!!

THAT WAS TOTALLY UNNECESSARY! WE CAN GET ALL WE NEED FROM THE GUYS I TIED DOWN!!

WE HAVE PEOPLE RAIDING IT RIGHT NOW.

BY FOLLOWING THEM, I FOUND THEIR HIDEOUT.

THOSE ARE HIRED THUGS... THEY WON'T KNOW ANYTHING.

WHA?!

SHEESH. OH WELL...

C'MON, UH...

FOLLOW ME IF YOU WANT TO KNOW.

IT ISN'T FAR.

IS MASAKI THERE...?

POS-SIBLY.

GOD, THIS IS AWKWARD.

"AKIRA" ISN'T A RARE NAME, BUT IT STILL FEELS WEIRD, SAYING IT ALOUD.

MY GRANDDAD WAS A BIG FAN OF KOBAYASHI AKIRA, YOU SEE.

ASAHI. THE ONE FOR SUNRISE.

WHAT KANJI CHARACTER DO YOU USE FOR IT? MINE'S AKATSUKI, THE ONE THAT MEANS "DAWN."

旭 = asashi   暁 = akatsuki

GRANDDAD AND HIS FAMILY IMMIGRATED TO BRAZIL SOME YEARS AFTER THE END OF WORLD WAR II...

"WREST YOUR VERY OWN FARMLAND, STRAIGHT OUT OF THE FERTILE JUNGLE."

THAT PROMISE HAD THE WHOLE FAMILY EXCITED. THEY WENT OVER, FULL OF HOPE AND DREAMS.

BUT TEN YEARS AFTER THEY ARRIVED, MY DAD AND MY OLDER BROTHERS ALL DIED, ONE AFTER THE OTHER...

TUBER-CULOSIS.

THE ONLY ONE LEFT WHO COULD WORK THE FIELDS WAS GRANDDAD. ALL THOSE DREAMS OF OUR OWN FARM ENDED AS JUST THAT, AS DREAMS.

LATE AT NIGHT, HE'D COME HOME AND SIT ME ON HIS LAP, HUMMING KOBAYASHI AKIRA'S OLD SONGS.

I STILL REMEMBER THE LONG DAYS HE'D SPEND, TILLING SOMEBODY ELSE'S FIELDS...

THE FAMILY STILL NEEDED FOOD TO EAT.

AND, EVEN BIGGER, WE STILL NEEDED TO PAY BACK THE GOVERNMENT LOAN THAT HAD PAID OUR SEA-FARE THERE.

GRANDDAD ENDED UP BEGGING FOR WORK FROM ANOTHER JAPANESE IMMIGRANT WHO HAD HAD MORE SUCCESS. AS FAR AS I KNOW, HE'S STILL THERE.

HEARING YOU HUM, RULI, REMINDED ME OF HIM.

EVEN NOW, I CAN STILL HEAR HIS GRAVELLY VOICE AS IF HE WAS RIGHT HERE WITH ME.

THEY WERE ALWAYS SAD, WISTFUL TUNES...

THERE IT IS.

OVER THERE.

IT'S FIN-ISHED.

WELL?

CAREFUL.
HE'S
STILL
ALIVE.

YEEK
!!

THOSE SUIT-CASES!

!

OH MY GOD... THIS PLACE LOOKS LIKE A SLAVE AUCTION.

IT IS SOME-THING SIMILAR.

WHAT DID THOSE SICK BASTARDS THINK THEY WERE DOING?!

WHAT THE HELL IS THIS?!

THAT IS WHAT WE CAME TO FIND OUT.

NOTHING, I SEE... KEEP TWO OR THREE. KILL THE REST.

F-FOR HER MAJ- ESTY...

FOR HER MAJESTY ...

DID HE SAY ANYTHING?

AND THIS GIRL IS THAT REALLY FAMOUS LEAD ACTRESS FROM THE TAKARAZUKA THEATER TROUPE...

THIS ONE'S FAMOUS TOO. I REMEMBER SEEING HER ON A LOT OF TEEN MAGAZINE COVERS.

HEY, LOOK AT THIS!

THIS GIRL IS THE IDOL THAT WENT MISSING LAST WEEK! I REMEMBER SEEING IT ON THE NEWS THE OTHER DAY.

THANK HIM.

IF HE HAD NOT RESCUED YOU, YOU WOULD BE AMONG THESE VICTIMS RIGHT NOW.

WHAT, THEY'RE CELEBS?

ONCE EVERYONE IS CLEAR, "CLEANSE" THIS PLACE.

TAKE THEM ALL OUTSIDE.

HUH?

DON'T TELL ME EVERY LAST GIRL HERE IS A FAMOUS SOMEBODY OR OTHER...

LOOK!

RIGHT.

HURRY... BOTH OF YOU.

ALREADY USED. I SUSPECTED AS MUCH...

YES, I HAVE RE-TRIEVED IT.

AL-PHONSE. YES...

PSHUUU

WHERE DID YOU DISAP-PEAR TO?

CHECK THIS OUT!

THAT MEANS MASAKI WAS HERE FOR SURE!

IT'S ONE OF THE VACCINE AMPULES.

SO THEY *DID* NAB HIM. HE MUST'VE ESCAPED IN THE CONFUSION DURING THE RAID.

DAMMIT! BACK TO SQUARE ONE AGAIN!

BUT VAMPIRES ARE KNOWN TO GET GREEDY... THE BIGGER AND MORE POWERFUL THEY GET, THE MORE THEY WANT TO HAVE BEAUTIFUL PEOPLE AS THEIR SERVANTS, ACCESSORIES EVEN, TO SHOW OFF.

HURRY THEM. IT WILL BE DAWN SOON.

I GUESS THIS PLACE COULD'VE BEEN A BLACK MARKET SUPPLIER OF THE HOT AND FAMOUS TO THOSE KINDS OF EGOTISTS.

COULDN'T SAY FOR SURE...

SO WHAT THE HELL WAS THIS PLACE?!

THE ONE THING WE DO KNOW IS THAT THEY AREN'T YOUR RUN-OF-THE-MILL THUGS.

IF THEY WERE, THERE'S NO WAY ALPHONSE WOULD BE HANDLING THIS PERSONALLY.

BUT ONE THING I DON'T GET IS WHY SLAVERS WOULD BE SO WORKED UP ABOUT THE VACCINE.

I'M JUST AS CLUELESS ABOUT THAT ONE AS YOU ARE.

NO WONDER EVERYONE IN THERE WAS SOME KIND OF CELEB OR ANOTHER...

THAT'S PRACTICALLY SLAVERY!!

ALPHONSE WILL PROBABLY TAKE CARE OF THEM.

UNFORTUNATELY, IT IS TOO LATE TO REVERSE THEM BACK TO HUMANITY.

SO WHAT'S GOING TO HAPPEN TO THOSE GIRLS?

LIKE HE TAKES CARE OF YOU?

. . . .

SHE'S FROM *FORTUNE IDOL.*

HAVEN'T YOU RECOGNIZED HER YET?

WHAT WAS THAT SUPPOSED TO MEAN?

WAIT, DIDN'T YOU SAY RULI WOULD'VE BEEN THE SAME AS THOSE GIRLS IF I HADN'T FOUND HER?

YES. NO ONE HAS EVER MANAGED TO WIN EVEN NINE WEEKS IN A ROW UNTIL VERY RECENTLY.

OH, I'VE HEARD OF THAT ONE. IT'S SOME KIND OF TALENT SEARCH TV SHOW. WIN TEN WEEKS IN A ROW, AND YOU'LL GET TO DEBUT ON A MAJOR LABEL OR SOMETHING.

HUH?

THIS SEASON, THERE WAS A SINGER EVERYONE PRAISED AS HAVING THE VOICE OF AN ANGEL AND THE SONG-WRITING SKILL OF A MUSE MADE FLESH.

I HAVEN'T ACTUALLY *WATCHED* IT MYSELF, THOUGH.

RULI.

HER NAME WAS RULI.

Chapter 8: Labyrinth

OOOH!!

WOW! I DIDN'T KNOW YOU WERE A MUSICAL ARTIST!

SHE REALLY WAS ON TV!!

THAT WAS JUST AN AUDITION...

I'M NOT. NOT REALLY...

WHAT'S WRONG?

......

BEFORE YOU, NO SINGER HAS EVER WON NINE WEEKS IN A ROW ON *FORTUNE IDOL*.

IF THAT IS NOT PROOF OF YOUR TALENT, I DO NOT KNOW WHAT IS.

IS IT REALLY OKAY FOR ME TO BE THERE? SHOULD I REALLY BE THE ONE WINNING?

I... I ALWAYS HAVE TO WON-DER.

DID THEY FORBID YOU TO BE A SINGER OR SOME-THING?

YOUR PARENTS?

ACTUALLY... I JUST WANTED TO SING SOMEWHERE WHERE MY PARENTS MIGHT BE ABLE TO SEE.

ISN'T WINNING A GOOD THING? I MEAN, YOU'RE TRYING TO MAKE YOUR MAJOR DEBUT, RIGHT?

THEY JUST... UP AND LEFT ME BEHIND IN THE APARTMENT ONE DAY.

NO. THEY COULDN'T.

A SOCIAL WORKER FOUND ME TWO MONTHS LATER WHEN HE STOPPED BY TO CHECK ON SOMETHING.

MY PARENTS ABANDONED ME WHEN I WAS STILL REALLY LITTLE.

OH MY GOD! THAT'S CRIMINAL NEGLECT!

BUT I COULD NEVER REALLY FORGET ABOUT MY PARENTS.

I DID LIKE SINGING...

THE CHORUS CONDUCTOR WAS INTO "HOLISTIC" TEACHING.

I LEARNED HOW TO SING AT THE ORPHANAGE.

IT'S CHILDISH AND NAÏVE, I KNOW...

．．．．．．．．

SO I AUDITIONED FOR THE SHOW. THAT'S HONESTLY THE ONLY REASON I DID IT.

MAYBE THEY COULD SEE ME AND FIND ME.

SO I THOUGHT THAT IF I COULD SING ON A TV SHOW THAT A LOT OF PEOPLE WATCHED ...

YOU AND I ARE THE SAME, YOU KNOW.

WHEN'S THE TENTH SHOW?

IT'S... THE DAY AFTER TOMORROW.

DID THEY FILM IT ALREADY?

WE'RE BOTH WANDERING AROUND LOST, TRYING TO FIND OUR ROOTS.

I SWEAR I'LL SEE YOU REVERSED BACK TO NORMAL.

AND THEN WE'LL GO AND FIND YOUR PARENTS. I PROMISE.

AKIRA-KUN...

HUH?

PERFECT! THAT'S PLENTY OF TIME!

ALL RIGHT.

PLENTY!

SHH...

WELL...

THOUGH, OUR FIRST PROBLEM IS FINDING MASAKI. IT LOOKS LIKE WE'VE COMPLETELY LOST HIS TRAIL AGAIN.

THAT WAS FROM HIME-SAN.

SHE SAID THERE'S SOME KIND OF BIG RUCKUS GOING ON DOWN IN ONE OF THE UNDERGROUND RESIDENTIAL AREAS.

YEAH...

YEAH, OKAY.

SO WHERE DO WE START LOOKING?

THAT'S MASAKI! NO DOUBT!!

I JUST HEARD THE SAME THING.

WORD IS HE WAS A SURVIVOR OF THE WAREHOUSE EXPLOSION.

SUPPOSEDLY, A MALE CARRYING A VIAL OF SOMETHING IS BEING CHASED BY A LARGE CROWD OF CITIZENS.

COMING!

RULI!

TP TP

WSH

WE NEED TO HURRY!!

THEN HE'S HIP-DEEP IN A PILE OF TROUBLE RIGHT NOW! WHEN VAMPIRES GO INTO A RAGE, THEY COULD DO ANYTHING!

GRAAAA

WHAT
THE--
?!

THERE!!

SHIT!
THIS IS
PRACTI-
CALLY A
FULL-
BLOWN
RIOT!

THAT'S
MASAKI
!!

JUST WATCH. I'VE GOT THE PERFECT GUIDE.

A SHORTCUT...?!

WE WON'T CATCH HIM FROM HERE. WE NEED TO TAKE A SHORTCUT AND HEAD HIM OFF.

THEY HAD AN ERRAND TO RUN, SO THEY WENT TO HAMA-SAN'S PLACE.

HEYA, JIJI! THANKS FOR COMING ON SUCH SHORT NOTICE. WHERE'S CLARA AND ANNA?

AKIRA-ONII-CHAAAN!!

YOUR "PERFECT GUIDE" IS A KID...?

YOU KNOW WHERE THAT IS?

I HAVE NEW INFORMATION.

OUR TARGET APPEARS TO BE HEADING FOR THE NEW RESIDENTIAL AREA THAT'S UNDER CONSTRUCTION.

DON'T LET HIS SIZE FOOL YOU. JIJI MAY LOOK LITTLE, BUT HE KNOWS EVERY LAST NOOK AND CRANNY IN THE ENTIRE BUND. YOU WON'T FIND A BETTER NAVIGATOR THAN HIM.

WE NEED THE SHORTEST ROUTE THERE.

〜〜〜

LET'S GO! KEEP YOUR HEADS UP, AND STAY RIGHT BEHIND ME. FALL BEHIND, AND YOU'LL BE LOST FOR GOOD!

THIS WAY!!

TMP

HOW FAST COULD HIS LEGS GO?!

HE'S STILL JUST A KID!

GAH!

NGH!

FWOOO

NO WAY...!

WHERE WE NEED TO GO, BY THE SHORTEST ROUTE POSSIBLE! DIDN'T I TELL YOU?!

WHERE THE HELL IS THIS KID TAKING US?!

PONK

TWITCH

SHF

BEO-
WULF
...

IT'S
BEO-
WULF!

THANKS.
WE
APPRECI-
ATE IT.

WHOA!
ONE
GLARE,
AND
THEY ALL
JUST
SCAT-
TERED!

NOT A
PROBLEM.
WE WERE
ALREADY
IN THE
AREA.

!

TUG

WE HAVE A PROBLEM...

ARGH!

WHO THE HELL ARE YOU?! WHERE'S MASAKI ?!

THIS ISN'T HIM.

HE WAS CARRYING THIS.

HE IS QUITE CLEVER, THAT IS FOR SURE.

SO HE SET THIS POOR SAP UP AS A PATSY AND RAN THE OTHER WAY, HUH?

ENOUGH SO THAT IT IS A PITY HE IS ONLY A HUMAN.

DIDN'T KNOW WHAT THE HELL HE WAS TALKIN' ABOUT, BUT IT GOT HALF THE CITY RUNNIN' AFTER ME!

I-I DON'T KNOW! I WAS SLEEPIN' IN THE GUTTER, WHEN SOME KID CAME UP AN' JUS' GAVE THAT TO ME.

THEN ALL OF A SUDDEN, HE STARTED SHOUTIN' AND SHOUTIN'. "HE'S GOT AN AMPULE!"

GUH... I KNEW I SHOULD'VE MENTIONED IT EARLIER!

SORRRRY.

IT'S OKAY.

HE WAS WANDERING AROUND THE FANGLESS APARTMENTS, LOOKING REALLY LOST. WE DECIDED TO HELP HIM OUT AND TAKE HIM TO THE POLICE STATION, SO HE COULD GET DIRECTIONS.

WE WERE ON OUR WAY THERE WHEN YOU CALLED, SO I CAME, WHILE ANNA AND CLARA TOOK HIM THE REST OF THE WAY.

I THINK I SAW HIM!

THE GUY YOU'RE LOOKING FOR IS A HUMAN?

WHAT?!

AH, WELL. THAT'S ACTUALLY REALLY GOOD NEWS.

LET'S GO SWING BY THE STATION AND PICK HIM UP. THEN WE CAN *FINALLY* BE DONE WITH THIS WHOLE ORDEAL.

YOU HAVE YOUR OWN POLICE STATIONS HERE IN THE BUND?

WE HAVE ONE, YEAH.

YEAH...

ANOTHER ONE BUSTED... HOW MANY MORE DOES HE HAVE LEFT? DOES HE EVEN HAVE ANY LEFT?

LET'S GO.

Chapter 9: The Fortress Guard

YOU'VE GOT TWO HOURS LEFT.

IT'S ALMOST 6 PM NOW.

HAMA-SAAAAN!

DRUNK TANK. NOT HERE TWO SECONDS, AND HE WAS ALREADY MAKING A REAL NUISANCE OF HIMSELF!

SO WHERE IS HE? WE WANNA SEE HIM.

GO ON BACK.

SIZZLE

YO! THERE YOU ARE.

AKIRA-ONII-CHAN!

AKIRA?

MASAKI. ABOUT DAMN TIME I FOUND YOU.

WELL, YEAH, BUT STILL... IT WAS HELL, MAN! HELL!!

DUDE, YOU WERE THE ONE WHO LEFT ME BEHIND.

AKIRAAA!! WHERE HAVE YOU BEEN, MAN?!

DO YOU HAVE ANY IDEA THE HELL I'VE BEEN THROUGH?! HOW COULD YOU LEAVE ME LIKE THAT?!

DAMMIT, WHO WAS THE LYING BASTARD WHO SAID BEING A VAMPIRE WAS GREAT?

IT'S TOTALLY NOT. THIS SUCKS!

THEY'RE GONE.

......

RIGHT.

HAD 'EM ALL STOLEN FROM ME BEFORE I GOT SHOVED IN HERE.

GONE?!

YOU STILL HAVE THOSE AMPULES YOU SWIPED FROM THE WAREHOUSE, RIGHT?

HAND THEM OVER! NOW!

SHUT IT. I DIDN'T HUNT YOU DOWN JUST TO LISTEN TO YOU WHINE.

SO, UH... WHAT ARE THOSE THINGS, ANYWAY?

HALF THIS DAMN CITY WAS AFTER MY HEAD FOR HAVIN' THEM...

YEAH. HE STILL HAS AT LEAST ONE OF THOSE AMPULES SOMEWHERE.

YOU SURE THIS IS THE RIGHT THING TO DO?

AKIRA!

SEE YA.

DOES IT MATTER? THEY'RE GONE NOW.

HEY, AKIRA!!

YEAH. NO INSULT, BUT IT'S LIKE I'M EATING PAPER.

IT'S... WEIRD.

I CAN'T TASTE A THING.

WHAT'S WRONG?

....

HN. A SIGN OF HOW FAR ALONG THE VAMPIRISM VIRUS IS GETTING.

BEFORE LONG, THE ONLY NUTRITION YOUR BODY WILL BE ABLE TO DIGEST IS BLOOD.

HEY, NO WORRYING!

I SWORE WE'D REVERSE IT BACK, RIGHT?

RULI!!

AS... AS LONG AS YOU'RE WITH ME, AKIRA-KUN, I FEEL I...

MORE THAN ENOUGH...

I MEAN, YOU'VE ALREADY TRIED REALLY HARD FOR ME, AND THAT'S ENOUGH.

IT'S OKAY. I WOULDN'T MIND IF... IF WE DON'T.

BE-SIDES...

YOU'VE GOT THINGS LEFT TO DO! WE'RE GOING TO GO FIND YOUR PARENTS, REMEMBER? NO GIVING UP!

I'M NOT THE KIND OF GUY YOU THINK I AM.

WE'RE GOING TO MAKE IT!

YOU! AGAIN! WHERE THE HECK DID YOU DISAPPEAR TO *THIS* TIME?

THIS BUILDING IS SURROUNDED.

GOT YOUR CELL?!

PHONE'S OUT! THEY CUT THE LINE!

WSH

DAMN. THEY MUST'VE PUT UP ONE HELLUVA JAMMING ZONE.

NO BARS! RADIO'S DOWN TOO!

WHEN WE FIRST GOT HERE, HE ASKED ME TO LET HIM GO TO THE BATH-ROOM!

TO THE BATH-ROOM!

HEY! WHERE ARE YOU GOING?!

HAAH...

HAAH...

RATTLE

RATTLE

TNK

TNK

MASAKI! OPEN UP!

LET ME IN THERE! MA-SAKI!

Chapter 10: The Rose in the Sky

SO THIS ONE MAGAZINE... STARTED DIGGING INTO MY PAST.

MY AGENCY LEAKED MY DEBUT TO THE PRESS.

MY DAD GOT DRUNK AND WAS KILLED IN A BAR FIGHT.

MY MOM WAS A DRUGGIE. HER BODY WAS FOUND IN A GUTTER, SOME- WHERE...

BOTH MY PARENTS ARE DEAD, AKIRA- KUN! LONG DEAD!

THEY'RE DEAD!!

THERE'S NO HOME FOR ME TO GO BACK TO... NO REASON FOR ME TO SING ANYMORE!

THERE'S NO ONE TO HEAR MY SINGING ANYMORE. THEY'RE ALL DEAD.

YES, THERE IS. YOU CAN SING FOR ME.

......

I... I MURDERED A MAN.

YOU TOLD ME YOUR TRUTH, SO IT'S ONLY FAIR THAT I TELL YOU MINE.

WHEN WE CAME OVER HERE, IT WAS JUST ME AND MY MOM. SHE HAD TO RAISE ME BY HERSELF. SHE GOT DOWNSIZED OUT OF THE ONE DECENT JOB SHE HAD AT A FACTORY. SO SHE STARTED WORKING AT A BAR.

THERE, ONE OF THE LOCAL YAKUZA BOSSES GOT... INTERESTED IN HER.

I BURIED THE BODY IN THE MOUNTAINS.

I BURIED THE KNIFE I USED THERE TOO. BUT THIS KNUCKLEHEAD WENT AND DUG IT BACK UP TO USE IN HIS OWN *STUPIDITY.*

I'M NOT A NICE GUY, RULI. I'M A KILLER WITH A SHORT FUSE.

I SHOULD'VE REALIZED THIS A LONG TIME AGO, BUT AFTER ALL THAT'S HAPPENED SINCE WE CAME HERE, I FINALLY UNDERSTAND.

EVEN *I* DON'T KNOW WHAT I'LL DO NEXT.

AKIRA-KUN...

I TOLD MYSELF I WAS ONLY ALONG FOR THE RIDE, BUT I THINK, DEEP DOWN, I *WANTED* TO COME HERE.

YOU RECONNECTED ME WITH MY PAST, WITH MY HAPPIER LIFE.

THINGS LIKE MY MOM, MY GRANDDAD, LIFE IN BRAZIL...

LISTENING TO YOUR SONG WAS WONDERFUL, THOUGH. IT HELPED ME TO REMEMBER A LOT OF THINGS. BETTER THINGS. HAPPIER THINGS.

THE CAVALRY HAS OFFICIALLY ARRIVED.

EXCEL-
LENT.

WE HAVE
SUCCESS-
FULLY SUP-
PRESSED
THE
REBELLIOUS
FORCE,
YOUR
MAJESTY.

THAT
ALLOWED
US TIME TO
CUT OFF
THE BULK
OF THEIR
ASSAULT.

SOMEONE
SENT AN
ANONYMOUS
TIP THAT
WE COULD
FIND YOU
HERE.

!

I
THOUGHT
YOU
GUYS
WOULD
TAKE A
LOT
LONG-
ER.

WELL,
THAT
WAS
QUICK!

COME.
WALK
WITH
ME.

SEEMS
LIKE
YOU
DID
QUITE
WELL.

SO
THIS
WAS
YOUR
DOING.

SHE SHOWED UP AT THE POLICE STATION LATE, BECAUSE SHE'D GONE OFF TO *DELIBERATELY* LET THEM KNOW WHERE WE WERE.

YOU LURED THEM HERE, DIDN'T YOU? WITH US AS THE BAIT!

THAT WAS YOUR PLAN ALL ALONG...

THAT WAY, YOU COULD BE SURE ALL OF THEM CAME AFTER US, RIGHT WHERE YOU COULD CRUSH THEM.

I SAW YOUR PEOPLE PICK UP THIS WEIRD CAPSULE AT THAT SLAVER'S PLACE.

DOES IT HAVE SOMETHING TO DO WITH THAT?

SO WHAT'S YOUR ANGLE?

WHY ARE YOU SO DEAD SET ON WIPING OUT EVERY LAST ONE OF THEM?

YES. I KNEW THEY WERE DESPERATE TO SILENCE YOU, SO I SIMPLY MADE USE OF THAT KNOWLEDGE.

VERY CLEVER. YOU'RE SMARTER THAN YOU SEEM.

SO YOU SAW THAT, DID YOU?

SHARP EYES.

THEY'RE NANOMACHINES.

YES, THAT IS EXACTLY IT. THAT CAPSULE CONTAINS THE "PIED PIPER."

BUT IT WAS RECENTLY STOLEN FROM US.

TO BE HONEST, *WE* WERE THE ONES WHO ORIGINALLY DEVELOPED IT.

WHOEVER CONTROLS THE PIED PIPER CONTROLS THE VAMPIRES IT HAS INFECTED.

TO PUT IT SIMPLY, THEY'RE DESIGNED TO DRIVE VAMPIRES INSANE.

REALLY... NOW I GET IT...

FOR HER MAJESTY!

OTHER-WISE, WHY USE THIS KIND OF ROUND-ABOUT METHOD?

DON'T YOU MEAN, "BEFORE HIME-SAMA FINDS OUT"?

WE BELIEVE THIS WHOLE INCIDENT WAS ORCHES-TRATED, IN THE END, BY WHOEVER THE THIEF IS.

RIGHT NOW, I'D RATHER THE TRUTH BE KEPT QUIET.

YOU ARE CLEVER. HER MAJESTY DOES NOT YET KNOW OF THE EXISTENCE OF THE PIED PIPER.

OUR OBJECTIVE WAS TO GET CONTROL OF THE SITUATION BEFORE THE INFECTION GOT OUT OF HAND.

I MEAN, THAT'S THE REAL REASON YOU SENT THAT CHICK WITH US, RIGHT?

IF YOU WANTED TO KILL US, YOU WOULD'VE DONE SO A LONG TIME AGO. YOU'VE HAD DOZENS OF CHANCES.

THE ONLY ONES LEFT ALIVE ARE YOU AND YOUR FRIEND. TAKE CARE OF YOU, AND THIS WHOLE MESS DISAPPEARS INTO THE DARKNESS.

FORTU-NATELY, EVERYONE INFECTED WAS AGREEABLY SELF-DESTRUCTIVE.

I JUST MIGHT TELL HIME-SAMA ABOUT THIS, YOU KNOW.

I AGREE. YOU ARE A VERY INTRIGUING PERSON. I THINK I'LL LET YOU LIVE.

AT FIRST, YES. BUT WATCHING YOU MADE HER CHANGE HER MIND, AND SHE TOLD ME AS MUCH.

UNDER-STAND?

YOU WON'T. HER LIFE DEPENDS ON IT.

BUT WHAT WAS ALL OF THIS ABOUT?!

WHO WAS THAT THIEF, AND WHAT ARE THEY AFTER?!

WHY THE VACCINE?!

DO IT WELL, AND I'LL CONSIDER YOUR DEBT TO ME PAID.

I MAY HAVE SOME WORK FOR YOU AT A LATER POINT.

A SMALL SQUALL BEFORE A MUCH, *MUCH* BIGGER STORM...

BUT I DO KNOW THIS ISN'T THE END. IT'S JUST THE BEGINNING.

WHO KNOWS? I'M NOT SURE MYSELF.

I SAVED RULi. I WANTED TO HEAR HER SING AGAIN.

YOU? NO REASON.

WHY DID YOU SAVE ME?

KEEP OUT

La sesta compagnia in due si scema:
per altra via mi mena il solvo duca,
fuor de la queta, ne l'aura che trema.

In two, the six associates part. Another way
My sage guide leads me, from that air serene
Into a climate ever vex'd with storms.
—*Dante's Inferno, Canto IV*

Epilogue: What a Wonderful World

HIME-SAMA DECIDED TO TAKE A BREAK, AND ORDERED ME TO GO AND WATCH THE SUNRISE.

NO, NOT YET...

HEY, AKIRA.

ALL DONE WITH THE INTERVIEWS?

AH.

YEAH. THIS WILL BE THE LAST SUNRISE YOU EVER GET TO SEE IN PERSON, AFTER ALL.

OH, WHAT WAS IT CALLED AGAIN? SOMEBODY TOLD ME THERE'S A NAME FOR THE LAST TWENTY-FOUR HOURS A PERSON HAS BEFORE TURNING INTO A VAMPIRE.

"THE TWILIGHT HOURS" OR SOME-THING...?

THAT'S IT.

A LOT OF PEOPLE SPEND THOSE LAST HOURS REFLECTING ON THEIR LIVES AS HUMANS.

FOR SOME, BECOMING A VAMPIRE IS DEPRESSING ENOUGH THAT THEY KILL THEM-SELVES.

YEAH.

GUESS YOU ARE.

SO I GUESS I'M GOING TO HAVE TO LIVE.

IF I'M DEAD, I CAN'T EXACTLY LISTEN TO IT, NOW CAN I?

WHAT DO YOU THINK YOU'RE GOING TO DO?

RULI'S LAST AUDITION IS TONIGHT, RIGHT?

THAT'S GREAT NEWS. THANKS.

I NEVER WAS A GOOD SON FOR MOM... I'M GLAD I WAS ABLE TO DO AT LEAST THAT MUCH FOR HER.

YEAH. IT'S BLIND LAW THAT THE SURVIVING FAMILY OF ANYONE WHO WAS *INVOLUNTARILY* TURNED WILL BE COMPENSATED. SHE'LL GET A YEARLY STIPEND STRAIGHT OUT OF THE TEPES FAMILY'S OWN COFFERS.

SOME EYEBROWS WERE RAISED OVER THE WHOLE "INVOLUNTARY" PART OF YOUR TURNING, BUT HIME-SAN PUT HER FOOT DOWN.

OH, YEAH! I ALMOST FORGOT. YOUR MOTHER *WILL* OFFICIALLY BE GETTING REPARATIONS AFTER ALL.

REALLY?

SHE SAID SHE WANTED TO EXPLAIN WHAT HAPPENED.

I TOLD HER SHE DIDN'T NEED TO, BUT SHE WOULDN'T LISTEN.

RULI SAID SHE'D VISIT HER...

AS SOON AS EVERYTHING SETTLES DOWN, SHE PROMISED SHE'D GO CHECK IN ON MOM FOR ME.

I'M THE LAST PERSON A GIRL LIKE HER SHOULD BE HANGING AROUND.

SHE BELONGS OUT THERE, IN THE BRIGHTER, WIDER WORLD.

I THINK, IF SHE COULD HAVE, RULI-CHAN WOULD HAVE WANTED TO STAY WITH YOU.

BUT... I'LL NEVER FORGET HER.

WE MAY NEVER MEET FACE-TO-FACE EVER AGAIN...

BUT I'LL NEVER FORGET HER AS LONG AS I LIVE.

OH, HEY! WHAT ABOUT THAT OTHER GUY?

YOUR FRIEND. THE ONE WHO STARTED THIS WHOLE MESS.

....

LAST TIME I SAW HIM, HE SAID HE'D PULL HIS FANGS AND LIVE QUIETLY WITH THE REST OF THE FANGLESS.

IT SEEMS LIKE WHAT HE WENT THROUGH THOSE TWO DAYS HONESTLY SCARED HIM STRAIGHT. HE'S A COMPLETELY DIFFERENT PERSON NOW.

MA-SAKI?

HE WENT WITH THE FANGLESS KIDS.

. . . .

IT'S FUNNY. HE WAS THE ONE WHO WANTED SO BADLY TO BE A VAMPIRE AND LIVE IT UP...

SERI-OUSLY? GOD, HE'S SELF-CENTERED TO THE END!

Y'KNOW, I'VE SPENT MY WHOLE LIFE WONDERING WHO I REALLY AM.

BUT GIVEN A TASTE, HE WIMPS OUT AND GOES BACK TO BEING AS CLOSE TO HUMAN AS HE CAN. I WAS THE ONE DRAGGED INTO IT, BITCHING THE WHOLE WAY. BUT IT LOOKS LIKE I'M THE ONE MOST SUITED TO THIS KIND OF LIFE.

HA HA. YEAH. THAT'S HIM ALL RIGHT.

HE KNEW THAT, NO MATTER WHAT, HE'D ALWAYS BE A FOREIGNER OVER THERE...

I THINK GRANDDAD, HUMMING HIS OLD KOBAYASHI AKIRA TUNES AND REMINISCING ABOUT HIS HOMELAND, UNDERSTOOD IT FROM THE BEGINNING.

IN BRAZIL, NO MATTER HOW WELL WE DID AND HOW MUCH A PART OF THE CULTURE WE WERE...

EVERY-ONE ALWAYS CALLED US "THOSE JAPANESE FOLKS."

IT DIDN'T HELP THAT MY MOM WAS PURE BRAZILIAN.

MY NICKNAME IN SCHOOL WAS "FOR-EIGNER." STUPID, ISN'T IT?

THEN THE ECONOMY GOT BAD AND WE NEEDED TO FIND WORK, SO WE CAME BACK TO JAPAN.

IT MAY HAVE BEEN GRANDDAD'S HOME, BUT ALL THAT WAITED FOR ME WAS SOME STRANGE COUNTRY WHERE I COULD BARELY EVEN COMMUNICATE.

AKIRA...

I WASN'T REALLY BRAZILIAN. BUT I'M NOT ENTIRELY JAPANESE, EITHER.

BUT WHAT HIME-SAMA SAID REALLY STRUCK A CHORD WITH ME.

FOR AS OF TODAY, YOU WILL BE A VAMPIRE! THAT IS NOW YOUR FOREMOST, AND *ONLY* IDENTITY.

THAT DOES NOT MATTER NOW. NEITHER YOUR RACE NOR YOUR COUNTRY OF ORIGIN HOLD ANY MEANING.

IT'S WEIRD.

WHEN I HEARD THAT, IT FELT LIKE THIS *FOG* AROUND ME HAD SUDDENLY BEEN LIFTED, AND I COULD SEE.

BUT NOW, I'LL NEVER GET TO SEE ANOTHER ONE.

REALLY? IT'S WHAT YOU WERE NAMED AFTER!

YEAH, AND THAT'S WHAT MADE IT FEEL SO EMBARRASSING TO ME. I NEVER COULD MAKE MYSELF WATCH ONE BEFORE.

I SHOULD'VE WATCHED MORE WHEN I HAD THE CHANCE...

DIVE IN THE VAMPIRE BUND

THE SHOW MUST GO ON

Dance in the Vampire Bund

READING ORDER

SPECIAL PREVIEW

DICTATORIAL GRIMOIRE

RRRK

WHAM

AH!

AAAAAH!

PATHET-IC GRIMM!

THE BROTHERS GRIMM TRAVELED ALL OVER GERMANY TO COLLECT THEIR FAIRY TALES.

MY ANCESTORS? THE BROTHERS GRIMM...?

YOU'VE ONLY YOUR ANCESTORS TO BLAME FOR THIS.

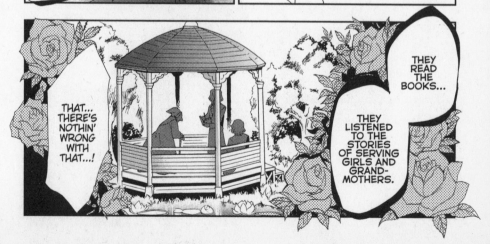

THEY READ THE BOOKS...

THEY LISTENED TO THE STORIES OF SERVING GIRLS AND GRAND-MOTHERS.

THAT... THERE'S NOTHIN' WRONG WITH THAT...!

THAT'S NOT THE TRUTH OF IT.

MANY STORIES WERE LOST THROUGH THE PASSING OF TIME OR IN THE CONFUSION OF WAR.

THEY MADE A PACT WITH US.

AND THEN THE BROTHERS GRIMM...

IN EX-CHANGE FOR TELLING THEM OUR STORIES...

THEY PROMISED TO GIVE US THE LIVES OF THEIR DESCENDANTS!

SOMEONE--

I'M GONNA DIE FOR A BUNCH OF FAIRY TALES?!

THIS CAN'T BE...

RRRK

Continued in *Dictatorial Grimoire Vol. 1!*